Ethereum

Mastering the Basics - An In-depth Look at Ethereum

Contents

Introduction

I want to thank you for choosing this book, *'Ethereum - Mastering the Basics. An In-depth look at Ethereum.'*

The world of cryptocurrency is now booming. Right from Bitcoins to Litecoins, cryptocurrencies have become the hottest property in the world of investments. One such cryptocurrency that has grown by leaps and bounds ever since its launch is Ethereum. Ethereum was valued at less than $10 at the beginning of the year and is now valued at $350. This makes it an absolute winner, and a must have.

If you are new to Cryptocurrencies, then you have come to the right place. This book will act as your Ethereum guide and introduce you to the world of cryptocurrencies. It will teach you about blockchain networks and mining. It will also tell you how to get started with Ethereum investments and double or even triple your money.

Let us begin.

Chapter One: What are Cryptocurrencies? An Evolution of Blockchain Technology

In this first chapter, we will look at the meaning of cryptocurrencies and Blockchains. The Ethereum network has its blockchain system where it stores data in the form of smart contracts. Now I'm sure this does not make sense to you, especially if you are a beginner in the world of cryptocurrencies. But as and when you go about reading this book, you will learn about these in detail.

What are cryptocurrencies?

In 2008, Satoshi Nakamoto introduced virtual currency known as Bitcoins. These were introduced to combat some of the challenges faced by fiat currencies. It was found that several banks were defaulting on borrowers' money and this was causing financial stress.

To fight such issues associated with centralized control, Nakamoto and his team decided to introduce a decentralized platform where people could exchange currencies without issues. Bitcoin was a cryptocurrency that could be bought and sold on the Bitcoin Blockchain. The Bitcoin Blockchain was a decentralized network where there was no central authority owning and guiding it. The power lay in the hands of the people, who could keep track of all the transactions that took place on the network.

Although the identity of Nakamoto was never revealed, Bitcoin was widely regarded as the best invention of the decade. Bitcoin continues to grow to this day and is valued at over $3,500. At the time of its launch, it was estimated at 10 thousandths of a penny. Those who invested in the coin during its initial stages have cashed in on millions, and their net worth continues to grow.

Bitcoins revolutionized the way in which trade was conducted over the Internet. It was easier for people to buy and sell using Bitcoins as compared to fiat currencies.

Features of cryptocurrencies

Here are some of the features of cryptocurrencies

Virtual

The first and foremost feature of cryptocurrencies is that they are virtual in nature. This means that they do not have physical existence and can only be bought and sold online. Once you buy the coins, they will reflect in your account.

Decentralized

The cryptocurrency network is a decentralized network. This means that there is no central authority such as government or central bank that owns it. The decentralized network makes it less susceptible to corruption and gives more power to the people.

Mining

Cryptocurrencies are mined and not minted like fiat currency. No government or central bank can decide and mint the coins. The onus lies on miners, who mine the coins by solving cryptographic puzzles.

Closed network

The blockchain network is a closed one and is cryptographically secured end to end.

Online wallets

Cryptocurrencies are stored in online wallets. In the same way as you have real wallets, cryptocurrencies have online wallets. These wallets are secure and will keep your currencies safe.

Universal

Cryptocurrencies are universal. You can buy and sell them in any part of the world. For example, you can buy them in Japan and sell them in China.

Legal

Cryptocurrencies are legally traded around the world.

Cryptocurrencies are gaining popularity owing to their consistent demand. Don't worry if you still haven't bought them as you still can make the most of them by purchasing now.

What are Blockchains?

Blockchain technologies are peer-to-peer networks where transaction data is stored. These technologies are secure and work as public ledgers.

In a day, thousands of cryptocurrency transactions take place. Since there is no central authority taking care of these transactions, the onus lies on a group of people known as Miners to make a recording of these transactions in the public ledger. The ledger is open to all and anybody can look it up thereby making it a transparent system.

Blockchains are now regarded as the hottest technologies and said to become the most used in the future.

Blockchain technologies are made using three types of technologies namely Private key, P2P Cryptography and Blockchain protocol. The Private Key gives people full possession of their coins. The key is a secret code that individuals must keep safe.

The P2P codes help people remain connected through interconnected nodes that allow them to authorize, authenticate and broadcast. The Bitcoin Blockchain is a public ledger that allows miners to make changes to the ledger. It costs a person some Ether to have these changes made.

Cryptocurrencies might only be eight years old but are bound to become the legal currency of the future. Experts estimate that they will come into circulation in 5 to 10 years and slowly displace fiat currencies.

Mining

Mining refers to keeping track of all the transactions that take place on the Ethereum blockchain. Mining is done to ensure that everything is running smoothly and legally. Miners are entrusted with the duty of keeping track of the investments and making sure that nothing illegal is going on.

They also help in creating the coins. Mining is now creating several opportunities for people looking for a lucrative parallel income. All it takes is a mining rig, and people can start mining the coins. Through the course of this book, we will look at mining in detail and explore the different aspects associated with it.

Chapter Two: What is Ethereum

In the previous chapter, we looked at the meaning of Cryptocurrencies and Blockchain technologies. In this one, we will look at Ethereum in detail. Ethereum is a blockchain system that produces the cryptocurrency known as Ether. It is regarded as Bitcoin's biggest rival and is soon said to over take its popularity.

Vitalik Buterin, who at the time, was just a teenager, launched Ethereum in 2014. He published the white paper on Ethereum in 2014, which was followed by the yellow paper published by Dr. Gavin Wood. Together, these two papers are widely known as the bible of Ethereum.

Meaning of Ethereum

Ethereum comes from "Ether," which means air in Latin. Buterin liked the word Ether and how it remains a permeable medium. He came up with the idea to name the Blockchain as Ethereum and the currency as Ether.

How was it created?

Buterin started researching cryptocurrencies when he was only 17. He extensively studied Bitcoins and co-founded the Bitcoin magazine. He wrote several articles on cryptocurrencies and Blockchain technologies.

After a while, he realized that Blockchain technologies need not be limited to Bitcoins alone and can be used to serve other purposes. He stated that emails are not the only use of Internet and extend to far greater uses. Similarly, Blockchains too can be used to serve other purposes apart from being a medium to exchange cryptocurrencies.

In 2013, he began working on a Blockchain model that not only allowed people to exchange cryptocurrencies but also host applications better known as Dapps. Once they came up with the Ethereum network and Ether, they decided to hold a 42-day presale for Ether in the form of ICO or Initial Coin Offering. This helped them raise 31,519 Bitcoins, which was estimated at $18 million and made for 40% of Ethereum. This money was used to pay off employee debts and contributed to the R&D team in Switzerland.

Ether is widely used within the Ethereum network and can also be bought and sold on an exchange such as Kraken. Ether is mined by miners who solve cryptographic codes to do so. Unlimited number of Ether can be mined with an average of 18 million per year. A new Ether is mined every 12 seconds.

Ethereum was priced just under $10 in January and is now priced at over $350. This means it saw a tremendous rise in value and is said to grow further.

It is Bitcoin's biggest rival and is meant to overtake its popularity in the due course of time. Many companies and experts have termed Ethereum as Bitcoin version 2.0 and considered it to be a higher and faster version of Bitcoins.

Smart Contracts

One aspect that is unique to the Ethereum blockchain is Smart Contracts. Here is a look at it in detail. Smart Contracts are computer codes that are used to facilitate the exchange of money, shares, properties, etc. As per smart contracts, a contract is automatically executed as soon as a particular criterion is met.

Let's look at a simple example. Suppose you and a friend enter into a wager over the price of Bitcoins. You say that the price will rise by 10 points in two weeks whereas your friend says it will fall by 10 points in 2 weeks. The same is fed into Smart Contracts. In case the price does rise, then the contract is automatically executed in your favor, and your friend should pay you the amount that has been decided. In case the price falls then the contract will execute in your friend's favor.

If this were to be carried out in real life, then neither you nor your friend would have made the effort of paying the other. Similarly, smart contracts automatically set off as soon as a particular criterion is met. This means people do not have to execute it manually. Most of the data on Ethereum is stored as Smart Contracts thereby making it an indispensable part of the system.

Dapps

The Ethereum network allows people to create apps on the network better known as Dapps. The Dapps will operate within the Ethereum network. Those designing the apps have greater freedom and can design using multiple tools. The apps will be released soon thereby further enhancing Ethereum's popularity. Building apps on Ethereum network will be quite simple. Anybody who has built apps for other platforms such as Android can be based on the Ethereum network.

Ethereum provides a decentralized web known as Web 3. It is different from Web 2 as there are no web servers and middlemen who come into play and demand commission. There is also no possibility of stealing and thefts thereby making the network a great place for people to build apps. You can go through the instructions provided on the Dapps for Ethereum website to get started with it.

EVM

EVM refers to the Ethereum Virtual Machine. It is a Turing complete software that runs on the Ethereum blockchain. EVM allows people to run any number of programs in any number of languages provided there is enough time and memory. This makes the Blockchain extremely efficient and fast. It also makes the system secure and prevents some of the issues faced by other Blockchains such as hacking.

As per EVM, there is a decentralized distribution of data into identical blocks, which is cryptographically secured at the highest level. This keeps it safe from Viruses and other cyber attacks. Ethereum is divisible and can be divided into smaller pieces. You need not buy the entire coin at once and can settle for a small portion of it. You can also make monthly investments in Ethereum.

Ethereum in banks

It is believed that some banks will soon start replacing fiat currency with Ethereum. It will be much easier for banks to keep track of the money and significantly reduce costs that are incurred in maintaining records. Blockchains are much safer and simpler to use as compared to traditional methods of bookkeeping.

A company known as R3 is currently working on blockchain models that can be used by banks. Their customers include HSBC, Barclays and a few other such global banks that are working on making it an available model. Once the Blockchain is designed, it will help banks keep track of the money that is coming in and going out and allow access to the public. This can solve the issues related to corruption and help sustain a better economy.

Updates

Ethereum is constantly updating and introducing newer versions. The very first version of Ethereum was known as Frontier. In 2015, a set of tools were introduced that could be used to create Dapps on the Ethereum network. The next version of Ethereum was named as Homestead and released on 14th March 2016.

The team is currently working on the next two models known as Metropolis and Serenity. They will also contain the apps that can be downloaded from the Ethereum network.

Chapter Three: Ethereum vs. Bitcoins

In the previous chapter, we looked at Ethereum in detail. In this one, we will look at the differences between Ethereum and Bitcoins. As mentioned earlier, Bitcoins were the first cryptocurrencies to be released. Although Bitcoins and Ethereum have multiple commonalities, they do have their share of differences.

Finding Blocks

The biggest difference between Ethereum and Bitcoins is the time taken to find a block. As you know, miners look for blocks on the system to solve them and receive a confirmation on the network. This takes about 10 to 12 minutes on the Bitcoin network whereas it takes around 14 to 15 seconds on the Ethereum network. This makes the Ethereum network faster and much more efficient. It allows miners to mine more in less time thereby making it lucrative. Ripple is an altcoin whose block time lies at 3.5 seconds making it one of the fastest in the business. However, the coin is not popular. There has been the talk of Bitcoin introducing changes to reduce the time taken to find a block, but there have been no such changes.

Infinite

Bitcoins will be limited in number. Only 21 million can ever be mined. This will make it easier to keep track of the number of coins that are in circulation. On the other hand,

Ethereum will be unlimited in number. Every year about 18 million Ether is mined. This means that it can be a little difficult to keep track of all the Ether that exist and can cause the Blockchain to slow down. However, the value of Ethereum will not go down and remain consistent regardless of the number of coins that are brought into circulation. It is believed that the number of Ethereum will very soon take over the number of Bitcoins in the market and can displace its market cap.

Cost transactions

The way in which costing transactions are carried out as per the Ethereum and Bitcoin systems is quite diverse. One is meant to set a gas limit to prevent running out of funds. The gas limit that is set is included into the blockchain by the miners. This block expenditure will be drawn out from the Ether that has been added to the account. If in case the system finds that there is not enough Ether present in the system then it will quickly abort the mission.

On the other hand, a Bitcoiner is required to manually calculate the fee that will have to be paid for the transaction and feed it into the system. This can prove to be a tedious task and make it difficult for the Bitcoiner to carry out the transactions. Experienced hands will be able to do this without an issue, but beginners will find it quite difficult. Many beginners end up making mistakes while calculating the fees. They will then have to abort the payment and make necessary corrections.

EVM

The Ethereum network comes with a Turing complete code, which means that any number of programs can be run on it in any number of languages, provided there is enough time and power. The code allows the computation of any function that is computable. This makes it a faster and more reliable network. The same is not a feature of the Bitcoin blockchain and can be much slower and a lot less reliable compared to the Ethereum blockchain.

Possession

Bitcoin was the first cryptocurrency to be released, and thus, there are a lot more owners. These were the first ones who mined the coins and bought them initially. Ethereum, on the other hand, was initially offered as an ICO and resulted in the sales of $18 million worth coins. Miners will mine about 18 million Ether per year while only about 7 million Bitcoins will be mined in a year.

Version

The Ethereum Blockchain was introduced in 2014 and has already gone through 2 versions. The Bitcoin was released in 2008 and still follows the same version. Ethereum was split into ETC much before Bitcoin was divided into Bitcoin cash.

As you can see, there are quite a few differences between Bitcoins and Ether.

Chapter Four: Advantages of Cryptocurrencies / Ethereum

Here are a few benefits associated with investing in cryptocurrencies / Ethereum.

Risk of inflation

One of the biggest benefits of investing in cryptocurrencies is that there is less risk of inflation. Inflation is a time when money loses its value owing to an excess of notes and coins being in circulation. This can lead to goods and services that are priced high forcing people to spend more and get less for the price. The central authority governing the currency can decide overnight and start issuing new notes and coins. However, this will not be a problem with cryptocurrencies as no central authority governs the issuance of coins and notes. There can be infinite Ethereum coins in circulation, and it will not go up or down in value. People will not run out of Ethereum to spend owing to the unlimited supply.

Acceptance

Often, when a new currency is introduced, many people tend to oppose it and do not accept it. For example, the new notes that were introduced in India were not readily accepted by people. This, however, is not the case with virtual currencies. People do not have to wait in lines or queues to be able to buy or exchange their old money for new. People also do not have to worry about any new rules being announced overnight.

The coins will not change in value or denomination and remain free from government and central bank control.

Safe investments

One of the biggest motivators of making investors is safety. It is evident that people will want their money to go into a safe place especially with the number of scams that take place. Cryptocurrencies provide people with safety and ensure that their investments are kept safe. Ethereum is usually bought and sold from trusted sources such as well-known exchanges. The Blockchain technology is extremely safe and free from hacks. Miners double up as vigilante and help in keeping fraudulent activity in check. It is also impossible to trace the identity of the sender thereby making it doubly secure.

Easy to carry

One advantage associated with cryptocurrencies such as Ether is that they are easier to carry. Imagine carrying around a million dollars in cash. You will end up sweating and probably drop the suitcase out of tension. Cryptocurrencies, on the other hand, can be carried in a Trezor or a USB. All you need is your private key, and you can carry around your entire investment. In fact, you can simply write it on a piece of paper and carry it with you. Nobody will even suspect that the piece of paper is worth millions.

No backtracking

One of the biggest advantages associated with cryptocurrency transactions is that the money cannot go back or roll back into the previous account. This can be a problem with regular money exchanges where the money can be backtracked into the previous wallet. This provides buyer protection and ensures that the transferred coin is not reverted into the previous account. The Blockchains also prevent thefts and double spending thereby making it a completely safe and secure place to conduct online transactions.

Growth potential

Cryptocurrencies make for excellent investment options for the long term. Ether grew in value quite drastically within a short period and continues to rise. The more people invest in it, the more its value increases. Ethereum and Bitcoin are now valued higher than gold, and their value will keep growing steadily. Buying them today can help you cash in on millions in due course of time.

Universal

Cryptocurrencies and Ethereum are universal in nature and can be bought and sold in any part of the world. The same cannot be said about fiat currencies as they change from country to country. One has to go through many hassles to exchange currencies. The rates remain the same universally.

Buying power

Cryptocurrencies come with a lot of purchasing power. You can buy from online sites such as Amazon, Overstock, etc. You can purchase a variety of things including furniture, jewelry, and groceries. You can also convert and exchange one cryptocurrency for another. For example, you can convert Bitcoins to Ethereum or vice versa. You can buy more with Ether as compared to fiat currency.

Transaction fees and costs

The transaction fees and costs on the Ethereum blockchain are meager to negligible. There are no middlemen involved; thus, there are no middlemen fees involved. This is unlike the stock market where broker fees have to be paid to complete the transaction.

Taxation

One issue that most investors have when it comes to investments is taxation. But do not worry, as the government has no say in your cryptocurrency purchases. This means that you will not be taxed for your Ethereum investments. You can invest all your surplus income into cryptos and save on taxes.

Open for all

The Ethereum blockchain network is open to all and anybody can keep track of the activities that take place over it. The system is quite transparent and will not allow any unwarranted transactions to go through. This makes it an absolute winner among people and helps in building up their confidence. All transactions can be immediately checked on the public ledger and can also be shared with others.

As you can see, cryptocurrencies and Ethereum offers a whole host of advantages thereby making it an excellent investment option.

Chapter Five: Shortcomings of Cryptocurrencies

In the previous chapter, we looked at the advantages associated with cryptocurrencies. In this one, we will look at some of the shortcomings.

Information

One significant disadvantage associated with cryptocurrencies is that there is lack of information. Not many people are aware of cryptos and their full potential. Many people are still not aware of Ethereum and do not know how and where to buy them. This is a primary reason why cryptocurrencies do not fare well with the masses. It is therefore important to educate more people about the currencies to get them to buy into it.

Business acceptance

Not many businesses accept cryptocurrencies as legal tender thereby making them less popular. Only a handful of online companies now accept Ethereum as legal money. If more and more companies start accepting it as legal, then it will grow much bigger and popular. In fact, it will be much easier for people to buy goods and services using cryptocurrencies as compared to fiat currency. People will have to shell out minor currencies to buy more.

Instability

One of the biggest issues faced by cryptocurrencies is instability. Some investors might think of this as a risky venture as the prices rise and drop erratically. This is owing to the high demand for the coins and low supply. As the demand increases, the price increases and can cause the value to remain high for a long time. News significantly impacts the value of cryptocurrencies and makes it rise or drop down within a small time frame.

Time to grow

Eight years might seem like a long time for cryptocurrencies to have existed. However, it is safe to say that the coins are still in their infancy stage and will take some time for them to grow in value and popularity. It can take anywhere from 5 years to 15 years for the coins to be accepted by the masses and pumped into circulation. It is safe to say people will have to wait for at least five years for their current holdings to grow in value over time and receive mass acceptance. The only way this is possible is through spreading the knowledge and ensuring that more and more people take to cryptocurrencies.

Mining

Mining has now become quite competitive and is forcing several miners to give up. Miners located in countries where electricity is cheaper are finding it easier to maintain their business as compared to those found in places where electricity is expensive. This can slow down the system by quite a bit. However, miners are now pooling their resources and trying to make it lucrative again. This can significantly help with keeping up with the system.

Speed

The Ethereum blockchain is much faster than the Bitcoin blockchain and can find a block within 10 to 14 seconds. However, there are newer cryptocurrencies on the block that are much faster and can find blocks within 3 to 4 seconds. This means that Ethereum should step up its game to recapture its audience. There are more than 600 Litecoins available in the market increasing the competition faced by Ethereum.

Exchanges

It will be essential to choose the right exchange to buy the coins. Most transactions today are trustworthy no doubt but will be best to pick one that is popular. Some of these include Kraken and Bittrex. Stay away from exchanges that are sending you unsolicited emails and asking you to sign up. These will be spam companies and might dupe you.

Safety

Although the Ethereum blockchain is extremely safe, there might be a few issues associated with safety with the websites that provide the wallets. Most of them are owned by third party websites and can result in a breach of safety. It will, therefore, be essential for people to exercise caution and only choose those sites where safety is given prime importance. It will be best to use 2A verification so that you know if someone is trying to access your wallet without your permission.

Private Key

One significant aspect associated with cryptocurrencies is keys. Keys are used to make currency transfers and are assigned to give your account a unique identity. These private keys should be kept a secret and not revealed to absolutely anybody. There have been quite a few cyber attacks of late where the keys have been compromised. You must beware of phishing attacks and not divulge details of the keys even if someone asks for it. There have been airdrop scams where people have ended up losing all their investments. You must ensure that the private key is kept safe and not lost, as that will mean losing your investments forever.

Transaction mistake

If you end up sending a coin to someone by mistake, then it cannot be traced back. This makes it extremely important for you to ensure that you have the right address to send the currency to. The public key should be entered correctly to transfer the coins to the right account. It will be best to personally send the coin to the receiver instead of asking someone else to do it for you.

These are some of the shortcomings faced by Ethereum and cryptocurrencies in general. However, with time and by being a little careful, one can reverse these issues and put a cap on them.

Chapter Six: Experts take on Ethereum

Ethereum has managed to garner an equal number of supporters and critics since its launch in 2014. The opinion remains divided over whether Ethereum is the best cryptocurrency to invest in at the moment. To help you understand this better, here is a look at the expert's take on the cryptocurrency.

In light of the recent drop in value that Ethereum faced, several experts brought the bar down on the currency and opined that it is extremely volatile in nature. Ethereum suffered an overnight fall from $300 to 10 cents creating mass hysteria among investors. There were rumors that it would not recover and would remain low. However, there were sections of cryptocurrency experts who were convinced that this was only a small hiccup and that it will be back to the top in no time.

Such falls are part and parcel of every currency and will continue to happen as long as the currency exists. Experts believe that it is wrong to call it a crash and was a mere technical snag. Once the snag was corrected, the value of the currency rose up once again.

According to the author of "The Business Blockchain," Ethereum is a much faster and better cryptocurrency as compared to Bitcoins and other Litecoins. It is much more reliable and can help people increase their investments through several folds. He stresses on the fact the Ethereum blockchain has much more scope than Bitcoin blockchain. It is designed to specifically help engineers build upon it and make it a bigger and better platform to help people exchange currencies. It is people's Blockchain and is popular among the developer's community.

He observes that several programmers have moved to the Ethereum blockchain, as it is better than the Bitcoin blockchain. It is simpler to use and faster in nature. It is also easier to build the apps.

Experts say that it is essential to give Ethereum a fair chance and allow it to establish itself in the market. It took Bitcoin 8 years to get to where it is now, and it is stable owing to consistent growth. The same is slated for Ethereum and is said to grow in value over time. Investors should refrain from writing it off just because it suffered a small glitch and give it a fair chance to grow.

Blockchain technologies have come a very long way since their inception and are bound to grow further over time. The entry of several new cryptocurrencies has made Blockchains quite expensive and now extend towards providing more functions than being just a platform to exchange the coins.

Experts rank the Ethereum blockchain much higher than other Blockchains and insist that it will be a matter of time before the blockchain grows bigger and better. People will forget about the dip once that happens and start investing in Ether. However, it is best to make your own decisions and invest in Ether only if you are convinced that it is a sound investment vehicle. You must weigh the pros and cons of investing to ensure that you capitalize on its popularity.

To help you make that decision, here is a look at the flipside of Ether and what experts have to say about it. There exist a small section of cryptocurrency experts who believe that Ethereum will lose its value over time. Ether will stop being the shiny new toy and people will swiftly move on to the next big thing.

Another issue that experts think will affect the popularity of Ethereum is that novices will not be able to understand properly how it works and what needs to be done to secure the coins. There needs to be more awareness on the topic to help people buy and sell the coins.

This lack of knowledge is contributing significantly towards keeping Ether's value low. Experts think that Ether has a lot more potential compared to Bitcoins and can grow bigger and faster in a shorter time frame.

The best way to deal with this would be by reading up on cryptocurrencies as much as possible and spreading the word about it. The more you speak about it the more you help the concept grow. Go through this book to understand the basics of the theory. But do not limit yourself to just this book and go through other books as well to increase your knowledge on the subject matter. You can also refer to websites to gain in depth knowledge on the subject.

Another issue that bothers Ethereum is its constant comparison to Bitcoins. This is only fair considering they are regarded as rivals. However, Bitcoins have been around for a much longer time compared to Ethereum. Bitcoin has been around for almost a decade now and has managed to establish itself in the world of cryptocurrencies. It has more brand value and stability s compared to Ethereum.

There are a lot more takers for Bitcoins than Ethereum at the moment as it has a bigger market cap. Any novice will first consider buying Bitcoins as compared to Ether. This should hopefully change soon and push Ether upwards. However, Ether is faster and can soon overtake Bitcoin's popularity. It has Smart contracts to its credit, which is a much quicker and safer option when it comes to Blockchain technologies.

Ether is secured at multiple nodes and can be used to make safe transactions. Bitcoins will be limited to just 21 million as compared to Ether that will be unlimited. Once all Bitcoins have been mined, they will come into constant circulation. This can make it a little difficult for Ethereum to survive, as it will have to compete against the biggest cryptocurrency in the world. However, some experts believe that the two can peacefully coexist without stepping on each other's foot.

Some experts think that those who already have Bitcoins will prove to be Ether's biggest consumers. This is because it is easier to buy Ether just by converting Bitcoins. One need not worry about adding fiat currency into the exchange to purchase the currencies. In fact, some exchanges exclusively accept only Bitcoins as a mode of payment and not fiat currencies.

One issue that is common among all cryptocurrencies is acceptance. Not many people will be able to accept cryptocurrencies as a legal form of monetary unit readily. They will find it difficult to move from fiat currency to cryptocurrency. It is also not accepted by most traders who still insist on having fiat currency as a mode of payment.

A segment of experts have scrutinized the working model followed by Ether and think that it functions in an inflationary environment. Ether is relatively new to the market and can rise and fall within a matter of hours. This gives rise to an inflationary market and makes it difficult to sustain consistency.

There has been news that POS will soon be replaced by new technology, which will put an end to mining. This will prove to be a big misstep, as several people will lose their job as miners. This has caused significant discomfort among the mining community who think Buterin should refrain from introducing the new technology and help them keep their job as miners.

One issue that is common among cryptocurrencies, in general, is that there will not be any buyer protection. There is no Helpline available that people can call for help. Once a person decides to buy cryptocurrencies, then he is on his own without any help from others. This can be a bit overwhelming to accept, especially those who are accustomed to receiving help from brokers in the stock market.

Although cryptocurrencies are decentralized in nature, there are a few countries that are doing their best to control cryptocurrency trade. This can hinder its growth and make it difficult for people to buy the coins.

It might also be a little difficult for people in underdeveloped countries to exchange their local currencies for Ether, as they will have to undertake exchange fees and interests that might be added by their bank.

Volatility

One of the aspects associated with cryptocurrencies is volatility. Cryptocurrencies are volatile to a large extent owing to the rise and fall in its prices. Experts believe that the volatility is a result of the speed at which the currencies are bought and sold. Many people tend to buy and sell within a short time frame that can lead to volatility.

One factor that can significantly impact volatility is big market players and scammers. There can be particular groups of people who pump in a lot of money into the coins and then sell them at once. This can have a significant impact on the stability of the coins.

An expert tip is to anticipate the rise and fall and be prepared for it. Do not panic buy or sell the coins and remain patient. If the price increases or falls then it will soon stabilize. There might be a few corrections that might be made to stabilize the prices.

Flash crashes are quite common in the world of cryptocurrencies. They tend to happen owing to technical snags. You must be patient with it and wait it out until the situation comes under control. If you panic sell during such times, then you will be the loser.

Remember that nothing is permanent in the world of cryptocurrencies. This applies to both the high phase and the low phase. The idea is to buy as many coins as possible when there is a dip in the prices. This can help you buy more at less price. A good idea is to anticipate the flash crash and be prepared to buy as many coins as possible.

For this, you must pay attention to the news and be aware of all things going on in the market. Subscribe to news and get timely updates from websites that will help you be on top.

Ether is sure to rise in price by the end of the year and might see a tremendous increase in value. It would, therefore, be wise to invest in it at the earliest.

Chapter Seven: How to Buy/Earn Ethereum

Ethereum makes for a great investment vehicle and can be added to your portfolio to strengthen it. But how does one go about buying or earning Ethereum?

Account

The first step of the process involves creating an account on an exchange to purchase the coins. Exchanges are places where cryptocurrencies are bought and sold. The account will be like a demat account where you log in to make the coin purchases. There are a plethora of exchanges available and can be used to buy the coins. Some of the best exchanges include Kraken, Bittrex, Coinbase, etc. You can choose the exchange depending on your analysis of the website. Once you choose the website, you must sign up with it. For this, you have to feed in your details and create a password. This password should be kept safe as you will be using it to enter the website. It will be best to choose a security code as well to doubly secure the account.

Verification

The next thing involved is verification. It will be mandatory to have your account verified to help you operate it. Each exchange can have its verification procedures. Some might ask you to upload documents that will serve as proof of identity. These usually include driving license or passports.

Verification can be instant or take a few days depending on the website. Once it is verified, you will receive an email notification and allow you to sign into the account.

Funding

The next step of the process involves adding in funds into the account. It is evident that you will require money to buy the cryptocurrencies. Fiat currencies are accepted and there is no limit to the amount that can be added. You can directly connect your bank account if you do not wish to transfer money into the online account. Some exchanges accept only stable currencies such as Dollars and Euros. If you have another currency, then you must first convert it to one of these currencies. IT will be ideal to know the exchange rates so that you know how much needs to be added in and how many coins it can fetch you.

Purchasing

The next step involves purchasing the coins. Once the money has been added to the account, you can buy the coins. Based on the prevailing rate of Ethereum, you can decide upon the number of coins to buy. If you happen to have Bitcoins, then you can simply convert them. Remember that you need not buy the entire coin at once and can simply buy a portion of it. You can make a monthly investment scheme where a portion of your income goes towards buying the coins. Once you purchase the coin, you must wait for some time until the coin appears in your account. You can check the ledger to see whether the coin has come into your account. You can convert your Ether into other Litecoins as well.

Download a wallet

The next step of the process involves downloading and installing a wallet. A wallet will be used to keep the money safe. Most of the exchanges do not make a safe place to keep the coins. The best thing to do is transfer the coins to a wallet. There are many wallets to choose from, and you can pick one that you feel works well. Once the wallet is downloaded, you can shift the coins from the exchange. But be careful while creating the account and make sure that you remember the password and the private key that you are provided. The private key gives your investment a unique identity and will help you keep your investment safe. If you wish to transfer the money to your wallet, then you will have to make use of the public key. You will require another person' public key to move coins to their wallet.

It is quite easy to earn Ether and here are two simple ways in which you can earn them.

Mining

One of the easiest ways of earning Ether is by mining them. Many people prefer this to buying the coins as it is simpler and can provide a consistent stream of income. You are required to set up a mining rig that will be used to earn the coins. The rig will help you find blocks that need to be solved to earn the coins. An average miner can earn about 1 or 2 coins a day depending on the speed of the rig. It will pay to use good quality graphic cards as they can reduce the time taken to find new blocks.

Payments

One other way of earning Ether is getting paid by clients. You can let your customers known that your business accepts Ether or you as an individual can accept it too. You can exchange something like a product or a coupon code to earn the Ether. That way, you can earn more Ether and avoid unnecessary costs associated with other modes of payment. You can also find out if your employer is open to paying you in Ether instead of fiat currency.

As you can see, it is quite simple to buy as well as earn Ethereum.

A note on keys

The world of cryptocurrencies relies on the concept of keys. These keys are unique identities that are given every individual account. Private keys give people a unique identity and help them carry out transactions such as buying and selling the coins.

I'm sure you have noticed the long string of numbers on a credit of debit card. These are meant to give the cards a unique identity. Once the cards are swiped, it tells the card provider which account to debit. Similarly, the keys are matched to determine the blockchain, which accounts to move the cryptocurrencies from.

The private key is a long string of numbers and alphabets. You must make a note of it and keep it in a safe place. Cold storage is best as you can maintain the information safe. The public key will be slightly shorter and must be shared with others to help them transfer the money to your account.

The keys are automatically generated and cannot be chosen individually. Remember that you must not share your private key with absolutely anyone. If you do then people can easily steal all your currency. There have been air dropping and phishing scams and will be best to be careful with it.

Chapter Eight: Types of Ethereum Wallets

As mentioned earlier, you must shift Ethereum coins to a virtual wallet to keep them safe, as exchanges do not provide as much security as wallets do. In this chapter, we will look at the different types of Ethereum wallets in detail.

Before we look at the kind of wallets to choose from, we will look at the two categories of wallets that exist. The first type is known as Cold wallets and the second category is known as hot wallets. Cold wallets refer to those that are not directly connected to the Internet. Hot wallets refer to those that are directly linked to the Internet. Although both can provide equal security, it will be best to choose the former as hackers will not be able to break into the wallets, and there is less danger of virus attacks.

Specific wallets

There are many varieties of wallets that are available and provided by third party websites. These wallets provide greater safety compared to exchanges, as their primary role is to act as wallets.

One type of wallet to choose is known as a particular wallet. These are specifically designed for individual currencies such as ether, Bitcoins, etc. They will be easier to operate, as they will be written in a code that matches that of the coins.

Myetherwallet happens to be a popular Ether specific wallet that you can use to keep the coins safe. Remember that the private key is an important part of the wallet and should be kept safe. If you end up losing the private key, then you will lose your currencies forever! There is no backup available, and you must keep it in a safe place.

One mistake to avoid when it comes to choosing a wallet is looking for ease of use. If you pick a wallet that is easy to set up, then you might end up compromising on the safety aspect. Make sure you opt for the 2A security so that you can keep your currency safe.

Desktop wallets

Desktop wallets refer to those that can be downloaded on your computer. Desktop wallets are quite popular owing to the ease in which they can be downloaded and installed. All you need is a computer and an Internet connection to set up the wallet. As soon as the wallet downloads, you can connect it to the blockchain network to receive the coins. Some desktop wallets to consider are Electrum and Exodus. Many people prefer this to other types of wallets, as it is easier to download and use.

Mobile wallets

Mobile or cell phone wallets are those that can be downloaded on your cell phones or smart phones. Mobile wallets are easy to download and easier to use.

Mobile wallets are alternatively known as lite wallets since they are easy to download and use. It takes less than 5 minutes to get started, and you can start using the wallet in no time. However, the problem with such wallets is that there can be a few security risks associated with it. It is easier for people to hack into the wallets. Phishing is also a cause of worry when it comes to mobile wallets. It will be best to personally overlook the transactions to make sure it is kept safe and secure.

Mobile wallets provide the feature of using QR code to transfer the coins. All you have to do is scan the other person's code, and the cryptocurrency will automatically transfer. If you are interested in having a cold storage to keep your Ether safe, then you can download the wallet on to a phone that you rarely use so that the coins can be kept safe. Since it will be a form of cold storage, hackers will not be able to get to it.

Mobile wallets come with more space, which means that you can store more Ether as compared to desktop wallets.

Physical wallets

Physical wallets are those that can be carried around physically. They are also known as Nano ledgers and can be used to store the cryptocurrencies. These hardware wallets are easy to carry around and can hold a lot of currency. Some popular hardware wallets include Trezor and Ledger Nano S. These can be a little expensive but will be well worth the investment as they are easier to carry and use. Another advantage associated with these wallets is that they cannot be hacked easily and can be used for many years.

Paper wallets

Paper wallets are a type of cold storage where a piece of paper is used to write down the private key and is added to a locker. This is a very safe way of keeping the private keys hidden and away from others. Cold wallets are much safer to operate and are free from hacks and viruses. Write down your private key on a piece of paper or print it out and add it to a locker.

These form the different types of wallets that exist, and you can choose whatever suits your needs the best.

Chapter Nine: What is Ethereum Mining

If you wish to get started with cryptocurrencies, then it is essential for you to understand the role of a miner and know exactly what mining stands for. Mining refers to extracting the coins from the blockchain network. As you know, the world of cryptocurrencies is decentralized, which means that there is no central authority such as a central bank or government that mints the coins and prints the notes.

The onus lies on the miners to earn the coins and pump them into circulation by spending them. Miner's help in keeping track of the transactions that take place on the blockchain network. Blockchains, as we know, are peer-to-peer networks where cryptocurrencies are exchanged.

It is a public ledger that is accessible to everyone. The ledger makes sure that no fraudulent activity is taking place on the blockchain network. This earns miners the title of vigilante, as they are there to keep an eye on the transactions and make sure everything is going smoothly. They are given the responsibility of making sure that there are no thefts and fraudulent activities such as double spending taking place on the network. These can develop over time if left unchecked on the network, as there is no central authority governing it. The miners make sure that all transactions are legal and oversee corrections as well.

The job of a miner is often compared to that of a banker. Miners maintain records of accounts just like bank managers do and maintain it in a virtual ledger. Since it is decentralized, the miner does not act as a middleman, and there are no transaction fees incurred. It is also a safer and reliable system as compared to manual recordings that are done at banks.

These coins are mined on the Ethereum network with the use of mining rigs. Let us find out how mining works.

What happens during mining?

Mining is a relatively simple process that takes place on the Blockchain network. Miners set up mining rigs in to mine the coins. The mining rig is connected to a set of nodes that are interconnected. Whenever a transaction takes place on the network, a block is formed. The block throws up a cryptographic puzzle that should be solved to earn the coin. This problem is solved by the miner through the use of a specific software.

Technically speaking, a miner runs a unique Meta data of the header through a series of hash functions. These hash functions are nothing more than random numbers and figures all strung together.

This metadata is made to run through hash functions and results in a change of nonce values and impacts the value that is created.

When this process takes place, the miner hits upon a hash value that can match the given target. If that happens then, the block is broadcast, and the miner is rewarded with an Ether.

The same block will be broadcast to all the miners, and only one will be able to solve it correctly. This means that the others should abandon their operations and move to the next block.

Finding solutions to the cryptographic puzzles is known as Proof of Work or PoW in the world of Blockchains.

The miner has to put in a certain degree of hard work to solve the puzzles and cannot cheat or make use of any special software. All miners are required to play fair and give everybody equal chances to earn the coins.

The Ethereum blockchain is quite fast and can find a block within a few seconds. This gives it an edge over the Bitcoin Blockchain, where it takes around 15 minutes to find a block. An average miner can earn a couple of coins per day if he is making use of quality graphic cards. The rig should be able to produce a sizeable number of Megahashes per second to earn the coins.

The number of coins that are mined also depends on the investment that has gone into setting up the rig. As an estimate, if you spend $20,000 on an Ethereum rig then you can mine around 4 to 5 coins a day.

You will have to buy quality graphic cards such as Radeon Rx series, which is considered the best one in the world. It can compute about 50 Megahashes per second, which is quite high.

But before you invest, you must understand that the miner's job might soon come to a close. Proof of Work will soon be replaced by Proof of Stake, which will shift the power into the hands of the people. They will be able to secure the transactions without the help of a miner.

Chapter Ten: How to Mine Ethereum

Now that you are aware of a miner's role, it is time to look at how you can start mining Ether. The Ethereum Blockchain is a virtual ledger where all the transactions taking place on the blockchain are recorded. If any mistakes or issues seep into the ledger, then the Miner makes necessary changes to it. This is done to keep the ledger updated. For this, the Miner is required to set up a rig that works 24 hours non-stop. This increases chances of finding more coins per day.

Do not worry if you are a novice at mining and do not happen to be an engineer. You do not have to be one to be able to set up the rigs and mine the coins. Once the mining rig has been established, it will start working on its own.

Mining systems

When setting up the mining rigs, it will be substantial for the miner to choose efficient systems that do not draw in excess electricity as this can lead to a big electricity bill to take care of. Remember that the systems will be running the whole day, every day, and so, you will have to buy energy efficient parts. If you live in a country where the electricity charges are too high, then you might have a tough time keeping up with the costs.

On average, you can expect to pay around $800 to $850 to mine 5 to 6 coins per day. This can significantly vary depending on the country that you live in and the average cost of electricity. Countries like China and India have cheaper electricity thereby making mining a popular hobby in these countries.

Here is all that you will need to set up the Ethereum mining rig.

Appropriate Hardware

The very first thing that you will require is hardware to set up the systems. It will be ideal to buy a computer that will be exclusively used to carry out mining activities. This will help you mine more.

You will have to make use of GPUs as compared to CPUs to mine the coins. CPUs can be slow and not be able to support the transactions. A GPU, on the other hand, will be quite fast and can help you mine the coins with ease.

The right GPUs can also help you solve the puzzles without much effort and in express time. As you are aware, you will be faced with stiff competition and must ensure that you use the latest technology to support the process.

If you have an idea as to which GPU is best, then you can go for it. But if you are unsure then do your research before buying the GPU. You will notice that the better ones are priced higher than the others. If you wish to make the most of your investments, then it will be best to go for the better ones.

Once you set up the graphic cards, you can connect the system to the screen. Some people find it easier to buy ready-made rigs, as they are easier to install and operate. They can be a little expensive but will be worth the investment. You can also opt for a second-hand rig, as they can be a little cheaper.

Some of the best graphic cards in the market include the Radeon Rx series and the AMD 6850. These can help you mine 2 to 5 coins per day.

Here is a summary of the hardware that you will require.

- A fast computer with a PCI-E slot
- 1 GB or more memory power to mine Ether
- A stable Internet connection that is reliable and will not hang during an operation. A minimum of 10 KB bandwidth will be required to support 5 seconds of mining
- 30 GB free space on a hard disk to mine more coins
- Ethereum mining software to mine the coins

The right Software

Once the hardware has been set up, it will be time to move to the software. You have to pick a software that is appropriate to mine the Ether. This is especially important if you wish to mine full time. You might have first to install a client that can support the mining software. It does not matter what operating system you are using, as there will be one for all.

The best software to use for Ethereum is Geth software that has been specially formulated to mine Ether. It is written in Go script language. Download the version that is compatible with your particular operating system and unzip it to run the file and install the software.

Once it installs, you can connect it to the nodes to start mining the Ether.

Test it out

Before you start using the system, test it out to ensure that everything is running smoothly. If there are glitches, then they can cause the system to slow down and affect your coin output. You can also connect the network to a system to mine dummy coins. This will tell you exactly how well the system works. But don't make it a habit of mining fake coins, as they are worthless.

What is the average time taken to find an Ether

I'm sure that you are keen to find out the time that it takes on an average to find a coin. Well, here is a simple calculation that you can perform to find the same.

You will have to first look for the target that has been provided to you on the blockchain. This target is a 256-bit number that is shared on the network Next; you must divide the target number with

115792089237316195423570985008687907853269984665640564039457584007913129639935

Once done, the resulting number will be the probability of a single hash that can be used to solve the block. Next, you can use the reciprocal of the probability number to find the number of hashes you will require to solve the particular block.

The resulting number should be divided by the hash per the second ratio to find the number of seconds it will take to solve a particular block.

Mining solo vs. mining pools

If you wish to be a solo miner, then it might take a little time for you to establish yourself and start mining the coins. Many solo miners tend to give up easily as they will not be able to mine a lucrative number of coins to offset the electricity bill that they incur.

In such a case, a miner, instead of giving up, can look for mining pools in his locality. These pools consist of a collection of miners who pool their resources to start mining in bulk.

Mining pools are created with the sole intention of helping the miners earn more coins per day. These coins are split equally among the members of the group or in predetermined ratios. This type of guarantee helps miners stick with mining and not give up on it half way.

If there are no such mining rigs in your area, then consider starting one of your own by inviting other miners to join in.

Geth

For miners looking for the best technology to install in their systems, Geth happens to be the number 1 choice. Geth is simple to download and can be set up on any system. Geth is a smooth running software that is free of glitches. This is an important aspect of mining software, as the software should work smoothly.

Hashflare

Many people will not be interested in setting up a mining rig of their own as it can prove to be a tedious process. Instead, they prefer to invest in a mining contract that can harvest the coins for them. This is easier to take up and much cheaper. One such mining contract is Hashflare, which provides cloud mining for Ether. Once the coins are earned, they will be transferred to your account. They also provide a calculator to help you calculate your profits.

Genesis mining

Just like Hashflare, Genesis happens to be a cloud mining website that helps people mine Ether. The leverage provided by the website is X11, which is quite lucrative. The mining contract can last for a year with the costs starting from $40.

Chapter Eleven: Ethereum Exchanges and Other Litecoins

If you are keen on buying Ether, then you must do so by signing up for an exchange. In this chapter, we will look at the different exchanges that exist in the market and help you choose the best ones.

Ethereum rotator club

If you are a novice or a beginner, then the best place to start is at the Ethereum rotator club. This website was the first one to provide an Ethereum faucet rotator and also happens to be the fastest. It is possible for you to earn a coin once in 5 minutes by covering ten faucets. The website functions smoothly and is designed to help you swiftly move from one faucet to another smoothly and efficiently. The website adds in high-quality faucets that are well paying and ideal for those who wish to start with a bang.

Poloniex

One of the best trading platforms for Ethereum is Poloniex. The exchange is quite fast, and one can buy Ethers with ease. Most people who use the website end up making use of the low price to buy the coins and sell them once the price rises. If you are adept at buying and selling stocks, then you will be familiar with the concept of short selling. The same can be done in Poloniex, where you borrow cryptos and sell them when their prices are high and buy back when their price drops, and return them to the original owner.

Bitmex

One of the popular techniques of trade in the stock market is futures option. As per this method, a person is supposed to guess whether the price of a commodity will rise or fall in the coming days and make an earning based on the result. Similarly, you can decide whether the price of Ether will rise or fall in the next few days. Based on your prediction, you can earn money from the website. There is no limit, and you can trade whatever suits your needs. The website offers one of the highest leverages at X33 for Ethereum.

Kraken

Kraken is the world's leading cryptocurrency exchange and possibly the best place to buy and sell Ether. The website is always busy with tons of people buying and selling coins on a minute-to-minute basis. You can use your Bitcoins to exchange for Ether on the website.

Bitfinex

Apart from Kraken, several other quality exchanges can provide you Ethereum. One such happens to be Bitfinex, which is based out of Hong Kong. The website is the third largest in the world and provides an exchange of almost all the leading cryptocurrencies.

Once you finalize the website, you can sign up and start buying the coins.

Some other cryptocurrencies

Bitcoin

Bitcoin is the world's largest cryptocurrency and also happens to be the first of its kind. Bitcoin can be purchased from all leading exchanges. Bitcoins can be converted to Ether.

Bitconnect

Bitconnect is different from Bitcoin and is an Asia based blockchain that acts as a peer-to-peer network to exchange coins. Bitconnect uses both Proof of Stake and Proof of Work software to help people mine and earn the coins.

Steem

Steem is better known as a social networking site for cryptocurrencies. It is a decentralized blockchain system that helps people exchange steem coins. Steem is coming out with Steem dollars, which will soon measure up to the US dollar.

Ripple

Ripple is a blockchain network that helps in mining XRP. The Ripple network is quite fast and efficient. This aspect has made the coin quite popular and earned recognition from banks such as Union Credit, Westpac and a few more. XRP is said to take off anytime making it a lucrative investment.

Monero

Monero is now known as a personal bank as you can control the transactions on it. It is quite easy to exchange Monero coins, as they are fungible. The coins can be bought by trading Ether on exchanges such as Kraken.

Chapter Twelve: Expert Tips and Precautions

By now we have gone through the world of Ethereum in detail. Now, let us look at a few expert tips and tricks to help you make the most of your crypto investments.

Treat them like stocks

For those who are wondering as to how cryptocurrencies should be dealt with then the answer is simple, they should be treated as Stocks. Just like how you would buy and sell stocks at a stock market, the same way you can buy and sell cryptocurrencies at the exchanges. They can also be treated as precious metal investments. In fact, Ethereum and Bitcoins are said to be more valuable than gold and silver thereby making them the better choice of investments.

Market share

What sets Ether apart from the rest of the cryptocurrencies is its market capture. Ether has a large market cap that helps with making it a crypto leader. Buterin's idea of holding an ICO for its launch paved the way for capturing a big share of the market. In due course of time, Ether is said to overtake Bitcoin's popularity and might overtake its market share as well.

Expert advice

Before you start out with your investments, it would be best to seek expert advice on the topic. For this, you can consult someone who has in depth knowledge of the subject matter. They can provide you with some valuable tips that can come in handy when you decide to make cryptocurrency investments. You can do your research as well and observe the particular currency's demand and supply chain to establish whether it makes for a sound investment option or not.

Message boards

Just like in the case of stocks, there can be message boards that exist for cryptocurrencies. These boards usually consist of investors who discuss cryptocurrencies and generate unnecessary hype. Such places can be breeding grounds for pump and dump schemes. These schemes encourage innocent investors to invest in a particular coin to get its price high. Once the price rises, a large group of people quickly sell the currency and force its price to fall. You must be careful of such schemes and ensure that you make the right investments.

Plan everything

Right from setting the budget for the mining rigs to the money that will be spent on acquiring the coins, it will be important to plan everything out in detail. Planning will allow you to take the right steps towards making the cryptocurrency investments. It can also save you from making unnecessary mistakes. Those who do not plan tend to give up too easily. This is not the right way to go about it as you might end up losing out on your investment. One good way of planning everything out is by consulting someone who has already made cryptocurrency investments and has inside knowledge on the same. They can guide you through it and suggest the amount that can be invested. Remember that it would be best to spend no more than 5 to 8% on a single cryptocurrency. This will spread the risk and help you reap sizeable profits after offsetting the loss.

Set yourself reasonable goals

One of the best ways to stick with mining or buying Ether is by setting yourself a few reasonable goals. Setting goals can help you achieve them and chase after your dreams. It will be ideal to set achievable time frames within which to attain the goals. It is also the best way to keep track of your money and chase after your dream of becoming a millionaire.

Maintain records

If you are just starting out in the world of cryptocurrencies, then it will be essential to go about it the right way. For this, it is best to maintain records of your investments and write down about your day-to-day crypto market activities. You can also create a watch list for the cryptos that you wish to invest in. This can help you stay on top of their price variations and make appropriate investments.

Following these simple tips can help you get started with cryptocurrency investments on the right foot.

Conclusion

I thank you once again for choosing this book and hope you had a good time reading it.

The main aim of this book was to educate you on the basics of Ethereum, and cryptocurrencies in general, and how you can get started with them. As you can see, Ethereum is now booming and will make an excellent investment choice. The key will lie in making appropriate investments. You can also choose to start mining the coins.

I hope you find success with your investments.

Good luck!

www.ingramcontent.com/pod-product-compliance
Lightning Source LLC
LaVergne TN
LVHW052321060326
832902LV00023B/4535